CW00327588

FOOTBALL'S

★ FUNNIEST ★ JOKES

Jim Chumley

Illustrations by Robert Duncan

summersdale

FOOTBALL'S FUNNIEST JOKES

First published in 2009

This edition copyright © Summersdale Publishers Ltd, 2014

Illustrations by Roger Duncan

All rights reserved.

Summersdale Publishers Ltd
46 West Street
Chichester
West Sussex
PO19 1RP
UK

www.summersdale.com

Printed and bound in China

ISBN: 978-1-84953-511-3

Substantial discounts on bulk quantities of Summersdale books are available to corporations, professional associations and other organisations. For details contact Nicky Douglas by telephone: +44 (0) 1243 756902, fax: +44 (0) 1243 786300 or email: nicky@summersdale.com.

To.......................................

From...................................

EDITOR'S NOTE

They say football is 'the beautiful game' but, as this book shows, it's a funny old one too. Here we have scoured the football pitches, terraces and commentators' boxes across the land to bring you the best jokes the game can offer. This collection of gags, guffaws and giggles will ensure you're never caught foot-in-mouth or score a social own goal again.

Telling jokes is a bit like playing football; you need to think on your feet, stay on the ball, hammer it in at an unexpected angle and know when to stop dribbling. It doesn't matter whether you support Red Devils or Wanderers, Spurs or Gunners; kit yourself out with this book and you'll never let the side down for laughs.

FEVER PITCH

'We've run out of salt and pepper in the club restaurant,' cried the head caterer.

'This happens every May,' replied the manager. 'It's the end of the seasoning.'

Why did the monk take up football?

He wanted to kick the habit.

A footballer lent his pencil tin to a friend, who was rooting through it and pulling out protractors and setsquares. 'What's this?' asked the friend, holding up a very complex-looking piece of equipment with lots of angles and lines. 'That's an offside rule,' replied the footballer.

There's only one ship that's never
docked at Liverpool,' explained
the dock worker to the tourists.
'Which is that?' asked one tourist.
'The Premiership.'

Who brings a rope onto the pitch at matches?

The team skipper.

The defender was clouted in the head during a tackle and knocked out cold. As the paramedic waved a towel at him and sprayed water on his face to revive him, he came round.

'Bloody hell,' he exclaimed. 'It was sunny when I fell over; this wind and rain's come from nowhere.'

'Can Timothy come down to the park for our game this evening?' asked Michael.
'No, he hasn't finished his homework yet,' replied his father.
'Well, can his ball come down to the park?' said Michael.

MANAGER'S BOX

The manager described his new
signing as a wonder player.
'Why do you call him that?' asked
a journalist.
'Because,' replied the manager
sadly, 'whenever I see him play I
wonder why I signed him.'

Two boys were caught scrambling over the turnstiles last Saturday at Wigan. They were given a severe warning and dragged back to watch the second half.

Reporter: Can you take free kicks with both feet?
Striker: No one could do that – if they were kicking with both feet, what would they stand on?

THE EASIEST TEAM FOR A MANAGER TO PICK IS THE HINDSIGHT ELEVEN.

CRAIG BROWN

'This is the deal,' said the manager. '£80,000 a month now, £100,000 a month in two years.' 'Great,' replied the midfielder. 'I'll see you in two years, then.'

'I can't believe I didn't score that penalty,' cursed the striker. 'I could kick myself.'
'I doubt it,' sniggered the opposition manager.

EVEN FERGUSON AND WENGER HAD THEIR RECURRENT WEAKNESSES; NEITHER, TO TAKE A COMMON INSTANCE, APPEARED CAPABLE OF DISTINGUISHING A TOP-CLASS GOALKEEPER FROM A CHEESE AND TOMATO SANDWICH.

PATRICK BARCLAY

Chairman: That was a pretty dismal game today.

Manager: Well, the crowd were behind me all the way.

Chairman: Were they?

Manager: Well, most of the way. I ducked down an alley and lost them before they could catch me.

STRIKING GOLD

The manager rings his striker and
asks, 'Where are you?'
'I'm in my garden,' replies
the striker.
'Did you know there's a match on
today?' shouts the manager.
'Yes,' says the striker. 'But you
said it was a home game!'

A local team in ancient Greece were three–nil up when the away manager called for a substitution. Their striker came off the pitch and on trotted a horse with the torso and head of a man to gasps from the crowd.

'Oh no, they're bound to score now,' groaned the home captain. 'They've brought on their centaur forward.'

Why did the footballer buy acne cream?

Because of his penalty spots.

DAVID BATTY IS QUITE PROLIFIC, ISN'T HE? HE SCORES ONE GOAL A SEASON, REGULAR AS CLOCKWORK.

KENNY DALGLISH

'Dad,' said the striker's son, 'can you finish my maths homework while I go and play football?'
'I don't think that would be right,' replied the striker.
'I doubt it would,' said his son, 'but at least it'll look like I've tried.'

SAFE PAIR OF HANDS

THE POPE WAS A SOCCER GOALKEEPER IN HIS YOUTH. EVEN AS A YOUNG MAN HE TRIED TO STOP PEOPLE FROM SCORING.

CONAN O'BRIEN

'Which position are you playing this weekend?' asked Jim. 'Are you in goal again?'

'I think I'll be in defence, actually,' replied Bob. 'I heard the manager say I'll be the main drawback.'

Why was the keeper sitting on the doormat?

He was waiting for the goalpost.

Why did the goalkeeper have so much money?

He was a careful saver.

POOR SCOTT CARSON. JUST TWO MORE HANDS AND ANOTHER CHEST AND HE WOULD HAVE SAVED IT.

JIMMY GREAVES

What do you call a girl
standing between
two goalposts?

Annette.

Who was the worst player
in the insect football
tournament?

The fumble bee.

GOING FOR THE CUP

Why is a successful football team like a lingerie shop?

It has a full range of cups and lots of support.

MAN OFFERS MARRIAGE TO WOMAN WITH FA CUP FINAL TICKETS. PLEASE SEND GOOD COLOUR PHOTOGRAPH OF TICKETS.

ADVERT IN CLASSIFIED SECTION OF A NEWSPAPER

What's the difference between the Invisible Man and Fulham?

You're more likely to see the Invisible Man at a Cup Final.

I'VE JUST NAMED THE TEAM I WOULD LIKE TO REPRESENT WALES IN THE NEXT WORLD CUP: BRAZIL.

BOBBY GOULD

A team of ants were practising
their free kicks on a saucer.
Afterwards, they retired to the
spoon for a team talk.
'Right then, lads,' said the captain.
'Big game next week – our first
time playing in the cup.'

TAKING IT FOR THE TEAM

What did the Scottish captain say to the referee when he asked if he had a coin for the toss?

'You can borrow this one, but I'll need your whistle as a deposit.'

'I've bought a Tottenham roving season ticket,' boasted Derek. 'Well,' replied Alan, 'I've got an InterRail pass. That's far better.' 'How's that?' asked Derek. 'You won't see much football with that.' 'Maybe not,' retorted Alan. 'But at least I'll spend longer than ninety minutes in Europe.'

Which team make more considerate lovers, England or Italy?

England; who else can be on top for nearly ninety minutes and then come second!?

**How do you save a
Manchester United supporter
from drowning?**

Take your foot off his head.

'My parents always beat me,'
sobbed little Johnny.
'Who would you rather live with?
Your auntie and uncle?' said the
social worker.
'No!' cried Johnny. 'They always
beat me as well.'
'Where can he live where he won't
get beaten,' asked the social
worker to her boss.
'See if there's any space up at
QPR,' suggested her boss. 'I don't
think they've ever beaten anyone.'

A couple had moved to a hut in
the Himalayas to escape from the
hustle and bustle of life.
'My football team lost their match
today,' said the husband sadly.
'How on earth do you know that?'
asked his wife.
'It's a Saturday.'

Why are West Brom like a piece of chewing gum?

They always find themselves stuck to the bottom of the table.

Why did the football club change its name to You Can't Play for Shit FC?

So it sounded like their fans were cheering them on.

A pirate took his parrot to the betting shop. When the football scores were being announced, the parrot looked up and said, 'Bugger it, Sunderland lost again.'
'That's pretty impressive,' exclaimed another man. 'What does he say when Sunderland win?'
'I've no idea,' replied the pirate. 'I've only had him for two years.'

HALLOWED GROUND

What did the manager do when the pitch became flooded?

He sent on his subs.

'This place is confusing,' the fan commented on the new stadium.
'Why?' asked his mate.
'Well, you're supposed to sit in the stands,' replied the fan.
'But you're not allowed to stand in the sits.'

THE ENGLISH FOOTBALL TEAM – BRILLIANT ON PAPER, SHIT ON GRASS.

ARTHUR SMITH

Why didn't the fans like the new stadium on the moon?

There was no atmosphere.

ON THE TERRACES

How many Grimsby fans do you need to change a light bulb?

All three of them.

Why are Cardiff fans like piles?

They're a pain in the arse.

The seven dwarves were driving to the Bolton match when they suddenly lost control and swerved down a bank, rolling the car upside down. When the paramedics arrived they feared the worst. 'How many of you are there?' they shouted into the wreckage. 'Seven,' came back the reply. 'We were off to the Bolton game. They're going to win the Cup today.' 'Well, thank goodness for that,' said one paramedic. 'At least Dopey's OK.'

WHY DO ARSENAL FANS SMELL? SO THE BLIND CAN HATE THEM AS WELL.

JOE LYNHAM

A man took his son to see Stoke City play. He gave the man at the ticket desk £40 and said, 'Two, please.'
'Certainly, sir,' replied the ticket seller. 'Would you prefer midfielders or defenders?'

'You look glum. What's wrong?'
'My wife's just had a baby.'
'But that's great news!'
'Not really. I've just watched my
football team lose 8–0 and now
I'll have to make my own
supper as well.'

FOUL PLAY

I USED TO PLAY FOOTBALL IN MY YOUTH BUT THEN MY EYES WENT BAD SO I BECAME A REFEREE.

ERIC MORECAMBE

What's the technical term for a Scotsman in the World Cup?

Referee.

I NEVER COMMENT ON REFEREES AND I'M NOT GOING TO BREAK THE HABIT OF A LIFETIME FOR THAT PRAT.

RON ATKINSON

Striker: Could you send me off if I said you were the worst referee I've ever known and my granny could do a better job than you?

Referee: Yes, I most certainly could.

Striker: What if I just thought it but didn't say it?

Referee: Well, I couldn't do anything about that.

Striker: I'll just leave it at that, then.

'You can shove that red card where the sun doesn't shine!' screamed the defender at the referee.

'Too late,' replied the referee. 'It's already full of three yellow cards and a corner flag.'

'I need a hobby,' sighed Tom.
'You should join the local football team,' suggested Brian.
'But I don't know anything at all about football,' protested Tom.
'Don't worry,' replied Brian, 'you could referee for them instead.'

Why did the footballer hate his Christmas present?

It had a red card attached to it.

TURF WARS

What happens after England win the World Cup?

The manager turns off the PlayStation.

'Where shall we take the team
on holiday this year?' asked the
Everton captain's wife.
'Let's go to Bath,' replied
the captain.
'Bath!' cried his wife. 'Why there?'
'They have open-topped buses,'
replied the captain. 'The
team never usually have the
opportunity to go on one.'

SHEFFIELD WEDNESDAY COULDN'T HIT A COW'S ARSE WITH A BANJO.

DAVE BASSETT

Which cartoon character supports Celtic?

Yogi Bear – he always manages to outsmart the rangers.

Ashley Cole goes into a bar and says, 'Just a half for me, then I'll be off.'

What's the difference between Accrington Stanley and a pencil?

The pencil has one point.

Why should you never run over a Liverpool fan on a bike?

It might be your bike
he's riding.

'Why do you always book two seats?' one Millwall fan asked another.
One is to sit on to watch the game,' replied the other, 'and one is to throw when the riot kicks off.'

IF EVERTON WERE PLAYING DOWN AT THE BOTTOM OF MY GARDEN, I'D DRAW THE CURTAINS.

BILL SHANKLY

If you're interested in finding out more about our books, find us on Facebook at **Summersdale Publishers** and follow us on Twitter at @Summersdale.

www.summersdale.com

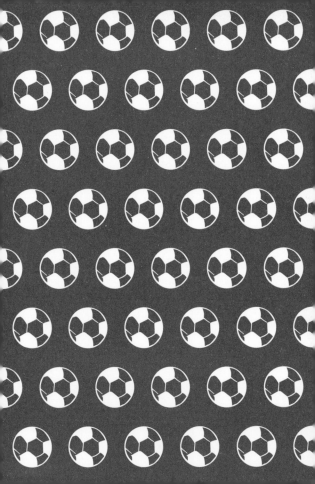

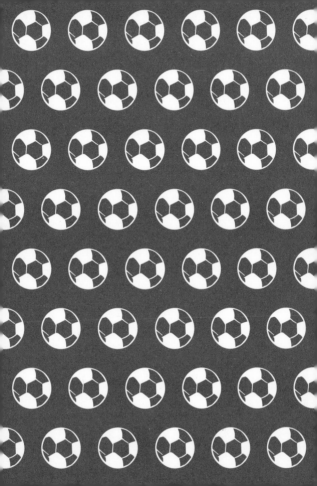